Speak to Manifest

A 6-Day Positive Self-Talk Challenge to Start Manifesting Your Dream Life

Law of Attraction Short Reads, Book 9
By Elena G. Rivers

Copyright Elena G. Rivers © 2021

All rights reserved. No part of this publication may be reproduced, stored in a retrieval system, or transmitted, in any form or by any means, electronic, mechanical, photocopying, recording, or otherwise, without the author and the publishers' prior written permission. The scanning, uploading, and distribution of this book via the Internet or any other means without the author's permission are illegal and punishable by law. Please purchase only authorized electronic editions and do not participate in or encourage electronic piracy of copyrighted materials.

Elena G. Rivers © Copyright 2021 - All rights reserved.

ISBN: 978-1-80095-093-1

Legal Notice:

This book is copyright protected—it for personal use only.

Disclaimer Notice:

Please note the information contained in this book is for inspirational and entertainment purposes only. Every attempt has been made to provide accurate, up-to-date, and completely reliable information. No warranties of any kind are expressed or implied. Readers acknowledge that the author is not engaging in the rendering of legal, financial, health, medical, or professional advice. By reading this book, the reader agrees that under no circumstances are we responsible for any losses, direct or indirect, which are incurred due to the use of the information contained within this book, including, but not limited to, errors, omissions, or inaccuracies.

The information provided in this book is for entertainment purposes only. If you are struggling with serious problems, including chronic illness, mental instability, or legal issues, please consult with your local registered health care or legal professional as soon as possible. This book is not a substitute for professional or legal advice.

Contents

Introduction 8

Making Friends with Your Inner Critic (and Why You Need to Stop Fighting it) 8

Day 1 18

The Biggest Self-Talk Secrets for Unbelievable Energy & Mindset Shifts 18

Day 2 39

Neutrality Tricks to Finding Ever-Lasting Inner Peace 39

Day 3 47

Success Starts In Your Mind, But How Do You Speak It Out? 47

Day 4 59

The Courage to Be With Yourself without Having to Change Yourself 59

Day 5 65

Making Friends with Your Subconscious Mind and Releasing Negative Patterns 65

Day 6 79

Affirmation Mistakes to Avoid and the Secrets to Manifest Your Dream Reality with Personalized Affirmations 79

Conclusion – Trust Yourself 96

Join Our Manifestation Newsletter and Get a Free eBook 98

More Books by Elena G. Rivers............................ 100

Introduction

Making Friends with Your Inner Critic (and Why You Need to Stop Fighting it)

It's not only about what we do, but also how we do it. In other words, it's all about the mindset and energy that we put into whatever it is we desire to practice, whether it's a self-development modality, spirituality ritual, or any skill we wish to master.

If someone asked me: "What is the biggest lesson you would like the readers to take from this book?" I would definitely reply: "My intention is that the reader fully grasps the concept that it's not only about *what* we do, it's also about *how* we do it."

Of course, there are several other beautiful revelations I recently had and am sharing in this book. But, once again, the methods and techniques you will discover in this book will not be as effective and transformative if you don't grasp the main principles behind them.

If you want to master your self-talk and use it as a manifestation tool to start living your dream life, there are several layers you need to embrace so that you can create a solid (and fun) foundation of what is next to come. And trust me, when you start living what I share in this book, your mindset and energy will begin shifting, and your life will start improving.

So, what are the layers that compose our positive self-talk mastery?

1. We are not *trying* to eliminate our negative self-talk.

Yea, bold statement, I know. I mean, we are supposed to be positive, right? This is a positive self-talk challenge, so am I losing my mind here?

If you are new to my work and haven't read any of my other books, don't worry. You don't need to read other books in the series to understand the principles of positive reality creation that I teach.

The main concept of positivity is this: never beat yourself up for catching yourself thinking negative thoughts, being in a negative mood, or speaking negatively.

The negativity that we experience is just feedback. Triggers can be healers. So, stop feeling bad whenever you catch yourself feeling bad!

Yes, of course, our primary goal is to be positive and keep shifting ourselves towards positivity. Embracing the art of positive self-talk is one of the best things you can do to live a better and happier life.

But, never try to shift towards positivity from a negative place of fear, such as: "Oh, if I keep being so negative, something terrible will happen, oh, and now I feel so bad about the fact that I keep having negative thoughts."

Instead, keep climbing the mountain of positivity daily, doing the best you can, and just moving forward. Do it because it feels good and because you are very excited about steadily climbing higher and higher, not because you are afraid or ashamed of where you are coming from.

In fact, as you keep climbing the mountain of positivity, you can allow yourself to look back, admire the view, and give yourself a pat on the back because you have come so far.

Keep this positive mountain metaphor in mind whenever you need it! Don't try to eliminate your inner critic because the power of your inner critic can be the biggest catalyzer on your journey. After all, it's thanks to your inner critic that you may be reading this book. You realized that your negative self-talk might be holding you back, and you decided to invest in yourself and take on this little challenge!

2. Release the "I need to improve myself" mindset.

Yea, I know, I know. We are all coming from the so-called: "self-improvement." But you see, personally, I don't like the term "self-improvement "because it implies we are not good enough. I prefer to define myself as a 'curious soul' or 'passionate about learning and growing.' Understand that you are good just the way you are, and reading this book and going through this challenge should be easy, exciting, and fun.

Imagine you are a little bit hungry, and someone cooks your favorite food. Your belly would probably be rumbling, and you might even start drooling. Finally! It feels so good. *I'm hungry, and now I'm gonna enjoy my favorite meal (and dessert). Yummy, I'm so much looking forward to it...*

Well, this is how your mind and heart should feel while reading this book and going through this challenge. It's supposed to feel like your favorite meal that a loved one is cooking for you to make you feel good, well taken care of, and happy.

Ask yourself: how do my mind and heart feel about what is yet to come? Are they excited? Because they should be!

And yes, I am not taking a typical self-help book approach with all those "you should do this and that." Instead, I use an intuitive and spiritual approach while taking action from love, authenticity, and joy for self-exploration.

So, remember, never feel bad about feeling bad. Negative thoughts and emotions are just feedback to remind us to keep climbing our mountains of positivity. And, as you dive deeper into the inner work that this self-challenge suggests, you will find yourself with less and less negative self-talk because your mind and heart will salivate (metaphorically, of course) at the mere thought of indulging in something positive. You will actually feel it, and you will look forward to exploring your inner positivity. Yes, we are naturally full of positivity, and we were born that way. It's just the rules of society that try to put us in our place: how can a person be so happy for no reason? Who do they think they are?

Well, the good news is that, deep inside, we are full of positivity, and we love it. It's just a question of getting back to our roots while unleashing our full potential. Our planet is awakening right now. We all need more and more positive leaders. When I say "leaders," I don't necessarily mean people in leadership positions. Authentic leadership starts with leading yourself while fully embodying your new, positive, love-based values and being an inspiring example to those around you (even if your work or profession doesn't involve leading other people).

To put it simply, everyone is a leader in my world, and I treat them as such. I believe everyone can unleash their positivity and add value to this world by raising their vibration and being a kind, loving and compassionate person. And this is the exact kind of reader I choose to attract!

3. Our inner critic is not always bad. In fact, it has good intentions because, very often, it wants to protect us from danger.

For example, knowing that I choose to eat healthily, my inner critic can tell me: "Hey Elena, drink water or a smoothie, instead of soda or sugary drinks. Remember? You promised yourself to live a healthy lifestyle."

This is an example of honest, uplifting self-talk. However, if I don't control what is going on, my inner critic may start abusing me with: "Oh, you can never stick to anything, all those empty promises! You just can't commit to anything. Oh, and I bet you will do the same with your writing, you will start and get all excited, and then you will just give up, as always."

As we can see, our inner critic is very talented when it comes to negative or even abusive self-talk. If uncontrolled, those things happen on autopilot. We end up speaking badly to ourselves.

Yet, we wish the world could treat us better. We want to attract people who are loving, kind, and compassionate.

Most people have ENDLESS negative chatter in their minds. And this is what blocks them from manifesting their true desires.
What good is it if you spend an hour a day scripting, affirming, visualizing (or any other Law of Attraction

method) if the vast majority of the time you're awake, you've got negative self-talk going on inside you?

Now, here's an exciting thing: *You don't manifest what you want. You manifest who you are and what you hold within you.*

Exploring and transforming your self-talk is one of the most effective self-development and spiritual tools to help you get closer to your desires (while enjoying peace of mind, happiness, and joy).

This is what this book is designed to help you with. You, too, can re-program your self-talk and become a conscious leader of your reality in six simple steps.

Remember the last time when you were unkind to yourself and pretty much abused yourself with negative self-talk?

Imagine another person treats you that way. You would probably feel sad and disappointed, and you wouldn't want to have such a friend. Or, imagine, you talk negatively to a friend. You would probably make them feel unhappy (and most likely would start feeling bad yourself).

But, for some reason, when it comes to talking to yourself (while accessing the biggest manifestation tool there is - your subconscious mind), you may assume that it's OK or normal.

Then, you may decide that you want to improve your self-talk or watch your language. And you perhaps enter into another self-imposed trap of: "Oh, I am not good enough, I need to change this and that, change and improve myself. Or, maybe I just need a list of affirmations and power words?"

Well, yes, there are some words that are more powerful than others and some words that are best avoided, and everything will be discussed in this book.

Remember the golden rule: it's not that much about *what* we do, but *how* we do it. So, what is the best *how*?

By now, you "should" know (kidding here, not my intention to keep "should-ing" you with things you should do)!

You see, I'm watching my language and words already. Since inner freedom is vital to me, I choose my words carefully. I also feel like communicating my message, not from a place of: "This is what you should do, this is good, and this is bad," but from a place of: "Let me inspire you so that you give it a go. See how it feels for you, and then you can choose for yourself."

So… what I really mean is this: intend to take action from a place of self-love, authenticity, and abundance. Do it to really embrace the power of positive self-talk while climbing your very own mountain of positivity. At the same time, love your inner critic, even the moments of occasional negative self-talk, because this is what got you on this loved-based journey of unleashing your full potential and raising your vibration!

Day 1

The Biggest Self-Talk Secrets for Unbelievable Energy & Mindset Shifts

"Your beliefs become your thoughts,
Your thoughts become your words,
Your words become your actions,
Your actions become your habits,
Your habits become your values,
Your values become your destiny" – Mahatma Gandhi

I remember seeing this quote so many times as a kid. When I was a little girl, I used to play at my friend's house, and her dad would always put positive quotes everywhere, even in the bathroom.

He was also an energy healer, which back then seemed very weird to me. To be quite honest, when I was a little girl, nothing seemed that weird to me, but I interpreted it as weird because my parents (both coming from a very religious background) would label those things as weird. Eventually, they decided I should stop playing with my friend and going over to her house because her dad was probably in a cult, did some energy rituals, and worshiped various thought leaders. Who knows what?

So, that childhood story entered my mind as soon as I came across that Gandhi's quote on social media, and I remembered that I first saw it in my friend's bathroom. I also remember her dad telling us so many times:
Never say: "I can't do this," instead, ask yourself: "How can I do this?"

In another situation, whenever something happened at a playground, for example, some kids would be rude to me, my parents would almost yell at me: "You see, you see, we told you! Why do you always end up in trouble?"
But, at the same time, my friend's dad would just say: "Hey, don't worry, it's all about learning. So, what have you learned about the playground today?"

He would also always tell us to never use words such as "Hate" and never call other people or kids "Stupid" to not create negative energy.

So, that was the first time I got exposed to positive self-talk without even realizing it. Unfortunately, my parents didn't see any benefits in my friendship back then, and so, as you already know, I had to stop seeing my friend.

Then, we also went to separate schools and didn't stay in touch. As a little girl, I used to feel a bit angry that my parents didn't allow me to go to my friend's house anymore, but now, I understand that they were just trying to protect me, based on their cultural and religious criteria and they were doing the best they could.

I even feel grateful for their decision because positivity, positive words, kindness, and positive self-talk are not something I take for granted. It's something I had to dive deep into and learn how to master myself.

I also believe that the Universe (the God, the Higher Power, Your Higher Self (or whatever force you believe in) sends us obstacles so that we can appreciate the good things in our lives. So, hadn't it been for my parents back then, I wouldn't have been able to experience contrast when it comes to understanding the difference between the positive and negative and the consequences of uplifting and defeating self-talk.

Your challenge for today is to take a closer look at the words you use. Remember that everything takes time, so never feel guilty about feeling negative or using words that don't fully align with positivity.

Your language patterns are fundamental, and there are many words I highly recommend you choose to let go of accordingly.

It may take some time, but it's worth it, especially when you start applying the tools from this chapter so that you know exactly which words to use instead.

We're talking about extremely powerful words that will make you feel confident and empowered while amplifying and speeding up the manifestation process.

For example, instead of saying:

"I am trying to,"

say:

"I am playing" or "I am experimenting."

To say that you "try" automatically allows the vast possibility of failure and even a lack of genuine commitment. For example, instead of saying: "I am trying this new business idea," I prefer to say: "I am experimenting with this new opportunity, or I am learning about it."

You see, when you experiment or learn, there's no space to fail.

When you experiment, you get a result that will teach you something. There's no such thing as a negative outcome; it's just an outcome, which is some kind of valuable feedback and data.

Instead of saying: "I want to," say:

"I choose to," or: "I intend to." Both are much more powerful!

Wanting makes us all wannabes. By definition, a wannabe wants something because he or she doesn't have it. They get stuck in the energy of waiting, wanting, and needing and never feel inspired to break such negative patterns with positive actions. If you're a pro at something, you already have it, and you do it. It's absolutely normal for you.

You can also say that you're "in the process of manifesting" something. Expressing that you are in the process is an excellent way to help you reduce resistance. This is extremely helpful if you set big goals and massive intentions, and maybe you get a bit nervous. If you state that you're in the process, it'll calm you down, almost on autopilot.

Move on with clarity and be decisive. For example, if you desire to become a successful entrepreneur, focus on one venture until successful. You can't be halfway in and halfway out.

By the way, I used to be a "halfwayer," lol, don't even get me started! But once I've made a clear decision and focused on my passion, things began to change, and I began manifesting people and circumstances that would help me.

Also, avoid "maybes" and "when I get this, then I'll..." thought patterns. Why not get there directly?
Maybe there's a direct flight?

Alignment is vital since you don't want to be in chaos vibrations or don't want to manifest "maybes" or "I'll do this when..." situations.

To be quite honest with you, I wasn't even aware of my negative language patterns and the way I spoke about my ambitions and desires until someone pointed it out to me. And that someone was my already mentioned childhood friend with whom I reconnected after many years. I was so excited we met again because she was a true embodiment of everything I desired, and she inspired me to transform my life. I soon began putting two and two together and quickly realized that my friend's success was also a by-product of her positive self-talk upbringing.

So, there we are, catching up and sipping on green matcha tea. And as I keep talking about my goals, my friend listens patiently, without interrupting me at all.

And I love it so much because, in my family, I would constantly get interrupted and reminded that money doesn't grow on trees and that I want too much.

Finally, my friend asks me: "Elena, may I tell you something? It's just a little feedback that I think can help you."

I say: "Yeah, sure, go ahead."

And she answers: "OK, Elena, first of all, I don't want to hurt your feelings or anything. I really feel like you have great potential to accomplish great things, but there are some negative patterns you need to release. OK, first of all, since the moment we met, you have been talking and talking about things you want to do. It was more like a monologue, not a conversation. You didn't even stop to ask me what I'm doing. But no worries, this is not a problem for me because I'm learning to be a good listener, so I'm grateful for that opportunity.

But, my point is, the way you spoke about your plans lacked confidence. The way you expressed your goals and desires, it seemed like you were trying to get my approval or someone else's approval or permission before you start. You also kept talking a lot about other successful people, but you weren't giving them enough credit for their accomplishments.

But then, you spoke about what you did, expecting other people to praise you and complaining about the fact they didn't value you. Finally, you kept talking about your goals, with a lot of words like *try* and *maybe* and *will see*. If I was you, the first thing I would do would be to start releasing negativity from your language as much as possible. Trust me, it will benefit you a lot, and your personal energy will shift. I also think it will help you a lot in the way you communicate with people. It will naturally open a lot of doors for you."

What can I say? Back then, my friend's words hurt my ego! I kept saying to myself: "Oh yeah, she can keep giving me her excellent advice, because she is Miss Perfect. She had a good, positive upbringing and better education. And now she's here trying to give me advice!"

But deep inside, something inside me shifted. I remember sitting in a hotel room after we met and thinking: "But what if she is right? What do I have to lose?"

I went out to buy a notebook to write in (back then, I wasn't a journaling junkie like I am now, so I didn't have anything to organize my thoughts). I got back to my hotel room and began writing my goals and ideas in a completely new way! This is how the exercise below was born, and this is how I started shifting my self-talk.

I warmly invite you to do this exercise and start talking to yourself using powerful words and language patterns.

Exercise 1:
It's time to re-frame your goals and desires...

Avoid saying: "I want to..."

Unless, for instance, you are ordering dinner, and you say: "Oh, I want this zucchini lasagne."
But, when talking about your goals, be assertive and say:

"I intend to!"

Oh, and be very mindful of using all those "buts."

Yes, you can say: "I wanted to go to the beach, but now it's raining," nothing wrong with that.

However, talking about your desired reality, dreams, goals, and ambitions is something sacred. So don't spoil that magic with "but's."

How does it feel to think about and talk to yourself about your goals using powerful words such as "intend?"

And how does it feel to replace all those "buts" with something more empowering, such as "I'm committed?"

Example:

Old, limiting self-talk: "I want to start a YouTube channel, but I don't have much time to do it, really."

New, empowering self-talk: "I intend to start a YouTube channel, and I'm committed to taking small steps to reach continuous growth."

Here's the next step you can take. When talking to yourself and reminding yourself about your goals, vision, and desires, attach your name to it. This will magnify the power of intention and take it to the next level!

For example:

"I, Elena, intend to write a new book on self-talk, and I'm very committed to my new desire; I absolutely love it!"

(BTW, compare it to: "Yea, maybe I will write a new book, but I don't know if people will like it. What if I don't have anything new to say?")

Now, please note, this book is not supposed to be about me. I simply use examples from my own life to illustrate my point and create actionable language structures for you to use in your own life.

For example, Nancy's goal is to start earning 10k a month in her new coaching business. And yes, she could torture herself with "maybe's" and "but's," and "it's hard." And for sure, the more you focus on the fact that the goal is challenging and few people make it, the more you program your Reticular Activating System (RAS) for it. So you will start looking for proof of why it is hard and get stuck in your old reality.

The RAS is what makes the Law of Attraction work. And it always works. It's totally up to you to choose to wake up and begin to consciously program yourself, scripting your life in the way you desire.

Your RAS registers what you focus on and creates filters to display what's on your mind. In other words, it uses its intelligent algorithms to show you precisely what it thinks you most desire to see.

There is a minor problem, though! While the RAS is good at showing you what it thinks you want to see or what drives your attention, it isn't great at understanding what you truly want.

It can only determine what you focus on - that's it. So ask yourself, what's on your mind? What do you feed it with? Do you focus on what you desire?

Now, back to our friend Nancy and her ambitious goal of manifesting a 10k a month business. She can choose to talk to herself in a highly empowering way and attach her name to her intentions. Example:

"I, Nancy, intend to make a consistent 10k a month income in my coaching business. I love my new goal, it's fun, and I'm learning and growing a lot!"

Now, what if Nancy experienced negativity and limitations coming from other people? Perhaps someone from her family told her she was no good or she would never make it.

Well, Nancy can also talk to herself using this structure: "You, Nancy, intend to make 10k a month in your coaching business; you, Nancy, are very committed. You, Nancy, absolutely love the process of achieving your goal."

Now, what if Nancy overheard some negative conversations about herself when she was a kid? Maybe a schoolteacher said something negative about her and how she was terrible with numbers, and then her parents talked about it, she overheard it, and it became her limiting story?

Well, she can also use this structure:
"She, Nancy, now intends to make 10k a month in her coaching business, and she absolutely loves it!"

Personally, I love inserting phrases such as "I love it" (or "you love it/ she loves" it whenever talking to myself about myself in the second or third person).

Some readers may be wondering if it would be more effective to even skip the word "intend" and just focus on the goal directly as if it was already achieved, for example:

"I, Nancy, am now making 10k a month in my coaching business, and I love it."

"You, Nancy, are now making 10k a month in your coaching business, and you love it."

"She, Nancy, is now making 10k a month in her coaching business, and she loves it."

And yes, this structure is also great. It all depends on how you feel about it. Some people may need a little "bridge," and using the word "intend" or "in the process of" can help reduce the resistance that some people may be experiencing while focusing on their desires.

So, it's really up to you which structure you choose to follow.

Another question you may be asking is: is this structure related only to our self-talk, or is it also about how we talk about our goals to other people?

The answer to that question is that it depends on who you are talking to and the level of connection and trust you have with them. It also depends on what motivates you.

Some people love making their goals public as it motivates and drives them to achieve them faster. If you love sharing your goals with other people, I highly suggest you start using empowering language while doing so because this is how you send out the vibration of confidence.

It is essential to mention that if you decide to share your goals with other people, you must be sure you can trust them and that they are kind, loving, and supportive.

You may even start your own mastermind group of like-minded people, where you help and support each other and positively talk about your goals while taking confident and inspired actions, embracing the process, and creating empowering, collective energy.

Personally, I don't share my goals with other people, except for friends who are on a similar journey to me and who I can fully trust. My reasoning for doing so is that I learned a few lessons based on my past mistakes (for which I am very grateful).

You know, I used to be a bit of a wannabe. I would get very excited about something and then talk about it with pretty much everyone I knew. Not only did I use all my creative energy to share my ambitious goals with others, but the way I used to talk about my goals lacked confidence, so I kept emanating this energy of a wannabe: someone who wants, is stuck in wanting, and that's it. And so other people would pick on this energy and eventually never take me too seriously. Back then, my self-talk was pretty negative, and I used to beat myself up for not even trying or giving up too soon. I was stuck in a negative pattern of wanting, chasing, and getting excited by some new shiny object again.

That was many years ago, and I have learned my lesson since then. And so, hence my new approach - I don't really talk about my goals unless someone I trust asks about it, or I confide in a trustworthy and experienced mentor or mastermind group while seeking guidance.

The interesting thing is that ever since I changed my inner chatter (and my inner world), my actions and behavior and how I presented myself in front of others changed automatically. My subconscious communication changed, even without diving deeper into studying body language techniques. And because of my new, transformed energy, I began attracting great mentors and guides into my life. At the same time, I stopped attracting all the negative critics and complainers who are just waiting to pick on someone and their insecure energy.

So, if you ever catch yourself feeling bad about the fact that you can't seem to attract the right people into your life, people who can help you, guide you, and support you, the first thing you need to do is to become your very own LOA detective and investigate your inner self-talk. The next step is to examine the way you talk about what you do in front of others. From my personal experience, sometimes less is more. The most successful and inspiring people I met in my life hardly ever talk about themselves and their accomplishments unless asked, or unless their story can serve as some kind of a lesson for others.

The bottom line is - it all starts with how you talk to yourself and how you treat yourself. You don't manifest what you want. You manifest what you hold inside. Your inner world translates into your behavior and energy.

Your behavior and energy are hugely responsible for what you manifest into your reality. While some people may find it a bit harsh, I think this is very positive and empowering. Remember what I said in the beginning? This is not about bashing or shaming yourself or others. And this is not about victim shaming or making yourself or others feel bad for what you manifested. People always do the best they can with what they have available. And positive self-talk is not taught in schools. I could beat myself up about that too. But, I choose to move forward while climbing my very own mountain of positivity. It's about true empowerment. Find the power within you. So, go through this chapter several times, if needed, to truly understand it.

When you're ready, take a piece of paper or a journal and think of your current goal or dream, something that really excites you and sets you on fire.

For example, let's say your goal is: "Make a living from my passion."

Re-write your goal using the following structure:

"I, Your Beautiful Name, am now making a living from my passion (and I love it!)."

If, for some reason, you can't really feel it and it seems too far away, and you feel like you are actually pushing it away, simply write:

"I, Your Beautiful name, am now in the process of reaching my goal of making a full-time income from my passion."

Finally, write your goal again, using the second and third person.

"You, Your Beautiful Name, are now making a full-time income from your passion."

"She/He, Your Beautiful Name, is now making a full-time income from your passion."

Use it as your personal affirmation whenever needed. Use it to remind yourself what your actual goals and ambitions are.

Exercise 2

Investigate your inner talk. How do you treat yourself? How do you talk to yourself when things don't go your way? Do you beat yourself up, or do you say: "Hey, don't worry, you did the best you could with what you had available. All is good in your world. Are you strong enough to learn and grow from this?"

Exercise 3

Write down at least 10 things you absolutely love and value about yourself. If possible, focus on different areas of your life, your accomplishments, talents, gifts, skills, and everything you love about yourself.

Compliment yourself using this structure:

"You (Your Beautiful name) are very good at…"

Or: "I love how you (your beautiful name) always manage to... (add activities you're good at)."

Examples:

"You, Elena, have a great sense of humor.
You, Elena, are very creative.
You, Elena, are passionate about learning."

Day 2

Neutrality Tricks to Finding Ever-Lasting Inner Peace

So, how are you feeling after the first day of applying super intense positive self-talk exercises? The first chapter of this book covered a ton of information to add the most transformative self-talk structures to your life.

I'm pretty sure you have experienced some massive shifts already. You should be proud of yourself and give yourself a pat on the back.

Yesterday was pretty intense, and we covered a lot of things. And today will be a little bit more chilled (but also very effective). Today, you will discover how to reduce the emotional intensity of negative words and self-talk using neutrality instead of negativity.

The main problem with negative self-talk is that it lowers our ability to see opportunities so that we can use them to transform our lives for the better. And the more we tell ourselves that we can't do something, the more we believe it.

At the same time, we are not trying to fight our inner critic and negative self-talk because it can create resistance, and what we resist persists. Imagine I tell you not to think about blue monkeys. Well, what comes to your mind? Lovely blue monkeys...

Today's lesson is short and practical and doesn't need long explanations. All you need to do is follow through with the following steps:

Step#1 - Give your inner critic a name or a nickname.

It can be a common name, or it can be something funny (maybe a blue monkey, if you think it suits your inner critic? It's kind of stuck in my mind for now, haha).

And so, the next time you catch yourself talking negatively to yourself, remind yourself that it's just that blue monkey talking to you. Be kind to it and thank it. Simply say: "Thank you for everything you do for me; I know you have good intentions. But now, I choose something different, something more empowering and something that works for me and my inner wellbeing".

Step#2 - Use words that slowly reduce negativity.

For example, instead of saying:
"I can't stand this," say: "This is challenging, but let me just see if I can find at least one good thing about it."

Instead of saying: "I hate this," say something like: "This is really not for me, but maybe other people will find it of value for them."

Instead of saying: "This is so terrible," say: "It looks like things aren't going as planned, but let's see how it goes. Maybe the Universe has a better plan for me."

Think of at least 5 negative things you told yourself recently and then re-write them. This simple exercise will give you your power back!

Positive self-talk is a habit, and a spiritual muscle can be built.

Step#3 - "Would you allow your best friend to get hurt" technique.

The next time you catch yourself with inner negativity such as: "Oh, I am so dumb," "Why didn't I do this on time?", or "I'm sure my boss thinks I'm so stupid," imagine that your best friend talks about themselves that way.

I'm pretty sure you would immediately react and tell them: "Hey, my friend, stop it now, you are not stupid, how can you say that? You are a brilliant and hard-working person, and everyone knows that. Don't worry. Everyone makes mistakes sometimes. Don't be such a perfectionist."

The main idea behind using neutrality to correct your self-talk isn't to ignore the truth or pretend everything is OK (while deeply inside still feeling bad). It's all about being more supportive of yourself whenever you make a mistake, just as if you would be if you were helping a friend, right?

So, it's not about denying we made a mistake while making excuses or blaming others. It's all about growing from our mistakes instead of just beating ourselves up over them.

Remember, you were not failing. You were growing and practicing for the bigger show! It's OK to acknowledge the pain, rejection, sadness, anger, guilt, or any negative emotion for that matter. Just do it mindfully and lovingly while thanking your older self for the growth it provided.

The final exercise for this chapter is to think of a mistake you made while trying to find at least 5 positive things you got from it. We're all human, and as such, we make mistakes. Some mistakes are lessons, some are blessing in disguise, and some are meant to make us stronger.

Example:

I quit my job to move to a foreign country, but it wasn't a good decision in the end.

Negative self-talk: "Why am I such a loser? Why I always make those stupid mistakes and make decisions without fully analyzing the situation? Who do I think I am?"

5 Positive Things Backed Up with Positive Self-Talk:

1. I had the courage to follow my way, even though it didn't turn to be my ultimate path, at least I had the guts to stick to what seemed the right thing to do back then.
2. Thanks to moving to a foreign country, even though it wasn't what I thought it would be, I learned a new language, and now, I'm pretty fluent at it, and I'm also happy I met new friends and can always go there on vacation.
3. I learned that I shouldn't make all of my decisions based on emotions and feelings. Instead, I need to find the balance between logic and emotions. In other words, I need to balance the masculine with the feminine to make better decisions in the future. Still, I give myself credit for having the courage to make such a spontaneous decision, even though it didn't work out. I'm glad I practiced it now while I'm still single and don't have any kids or family to support. I just had to learn my lesson to understand that spontaneous decisions based on fleeting feelings are not always beneficial for my future.

4. Thanks to quitting my job back then, I finally embarked on a path of entrepreneurship, and I also had to learn a ton of new skills that now make me a more valuable person in the marketplace. Plus, I strengthened my mindset and improved my habits, work ethic, and energy.
5. I finally learned to be humble and grateful and stop talking left and right about the things I'm gonna do. Because of the fact that after quitting my job, I bragged to everyone how I'm gonna make it abroad and be super successful, and eventually, I didn't make it; I had to re-evaluate my behavior towards people. Now I never brag about anything, especially about things that didn't even happen yet, because it creates bad energy and is not very kind towards other people.

One of the reasons I used to brag is that I felt insecure, so I might have made other people insecure. Now, I finally learned to be humble and be myself, and I appreciate that in others.

Can you see how positive self-talk can help you shift your perspective? Now, finish this chapter on a positive note and think of a similar situation or mistake from your life and then, find at least 5 positive things about it and back it up with kind and encouraging words.

This simple exercise will also help you change how you see and treat other people and be more compassionate towards others.

If you want to take this exercise to the next level, share it with a friend who is on a guilt trip and help them shift their perspective too. We can replace blaming with learning. Kindness matters, and it all starts with being kind to yourself from within yourself. After all, this is what and how we manifest. We manifest what we hold inside us. If you're on a path of spiritual development and you're seeking inner peace, be sure to come back to this short chapter whenever needed. The more you read it, and the more you go through it using different situations or so-called "mistakes" or "failures" from your life (or lives of others if you feel sorry for them and wish to help them), the more peace and growth you will find. You don't fail. You succeed, or you learn!

Day 3

Success Starts In Your Mind, But How Do You Speak It Out?

When I first started my writing journey, I was on a meager income and lived in a not-so-good neighborhood. Everybody would tell me I was crazy and I would never make it. Some would say it's because I lacked the discipline, some would say I would give up, and some would say I didn't have enough creativity or experience.

But here's the thing, because of all the inner work I had done before commencing on my journey, and also because of many amazing authors, coaches, and other mind experts who helped me heal my mindset and emotions, I already knew three things:

1. Most of the people who criticized my efforts were just trying to protect me from failure and disappointment, and so even though they seemed negative, they had good intentions.

2. Some of those people were simply projecting their own insecurities as well as past failures, unprocessed traumas, and disappointments.

3. And some were talking, and they really didn't have much idea about what I was doing.

The funny part is that I recently caught myself doing pretty much the same thing, actually. A friend of mine spent quite some time studying trading and investing, and now he's ready to dive all in. And I started telling him how risky it all was and that he should stay away from "all that stuff."

And he asked me: "But Elena do you know anything about trading or investing at all? Have you ever done it yourself? Yes, of course, there is some risk involved. I have done my research. I know how the best investors think. I know that I can only invest what I can afford to lose and never invest all my savings, hoping for some overnight miracle. I'm not getting into any get-rich-quick schemes. And I know that business involves risk. I mean, come on, you should know this, you are an entrepreneur. Besides, you know I never jump into things without doing any research and that I am all for diversification, and I have mentors I can trust. But hey, I appreciate you caring about me. I know you have good intentions!"

So, that kind of put me in my place (in a good and loving way, of course). And this situation also taught me something about trust and made me ask myself: what levels of faith do I have in myself and others?

I believe there is a connection between how we talk to others and how we talk to ourselves. There's also a connection between how others speak to us and how we speak to ourselves. No matter what the situation is, it seems like in the end, it all comes back to us and the way we treat ourselves and talk to ourselves.

Now, I'm no saint. Although I have done a ton of inner work, that work is always in progress. So, whenever I find myself thinking or speaking doubtful, negative, or criticizing thoughts towards others, I immediately ask myself: "Hmm, Elena, what does this say about your self-talk? What kind of doubts are you holding within yourself?"

Now, back to my writing journey and all those nay-sayers... I quickly realized I could not control what they think or say. Nor did I want to get in the energy of: "I'm gonna show them, I am gonna be the best of the best just to prove them wrong!"

(Well, it may work as a motivational factor for some people in the beginning, but acting from the energy of "I need to prove them wrong" never worked for me long-term).

So, I made a commitment to myself and my self-talk. I got involved in kind and loving conversations with my deep inner mind.

I had a deep faith in myself and my process, and so it fueled my writing. I remember so many people telling me I couldn't do it, but since I was so immersed in my mission and process, I knew that it was just a question of consistency, work, and focus in every cell of my body.

In my mind, my idea was that I was going to put one foot in front of the other and just keep going. Every day I looked myself in the mirror and congratulated myself on the steps I had taken. It quickly became a habit. Whenever I looked in the mirror or did my hair or make-up – I would just automatically start talking to myself and saying: "I love you no matter what." I also kept calling myself a prolific writer. Even though I didn't have any substantial success to show initially, I quickly noticed that the way other people perceived and treated me began to shift pretty soon. I remember a family member who would always call me lazy and disorganized once called me out of the blue and said, "Wow, what you do is so inspiring! You are a writing machine! I think I'm gonna write my own book too! You just showed everyone that everything is possible with hard work and consistency. I used to say some nasty things about you but guess what? I wasn't right. And I was negative. You also inspired me to be more positive because it looks like you can't go wrong with that. I know I'm ready to change my life. I am so excited, thank you!"

At that time, I also intuitively began doing mirror work without even knowing what it was! I only researched it later when I was studying Louise Hay and her books. Just talking to myself kindly and looking at myself in the mirror and saying, "You are doing great!" helped me tremendously, as simple as it may seem.

It took me a while to figure out this simple formula:

- Figure out who you are and what you really want.

- Define it and be kind to yourself.

- Fully believe in it and embody it.

- Think and act as if you were that person already.

- Do not expect approval, and don't seek it. Approve yourself and adjust your inner world accordingly.

Talking to yourself as if you were your own positive coach and mentor is the best way to keep moving forward every day!

Sooner or later, other people will start perceiving you as a leader, someone who is magnetic, intelligent, and unique. In other words, whatever you created within yourself internally, and whatever friendly and kind words you told yourself (mirror work helps a lot!), those around you will sooner or later catch on.

I gave up seeking approval and validation, and I approved and validated myself. Eventually, my reality began reflecting my attitude, and even people who would constantly criticize me suddenly became kinder towards me.

You can use this positive self-talk technique in any area of your life. If you want to create a self-image of someone who enjoys eating healthy food and exercising and sees yourself as such, you will be successful on your health and weight loss journey, even before you get started on your new process. Be the first one to acknowledge yourself. And team up with your subconscious mind by using the following structure: "We are doing great, we are a team, we work together, together we are unstoppable, it's safe for us to work together."

Whatever goal you set for yourself, you can achieve, but first, make sure that your self-talk supports your true authentic confidence and that everything is aligned.

Your Exercise for Today:

- Take a piece of paper or a journal and write down at least ten nice things you can tell you to be your own cheerleader and support your current goals. Whenever you see yourself in a mirror, look yourself in the eyes, smile, and tell yourself: "I love you no matter what!"

- Then, tell yourself how good you are already at whatever it is you're working towards. Acknowledge any small steps on your journey. For example, be happy and grateful that you called that prospect, wrote an outline for your book, or made a video for your website.

It's always those tiny steps that lead to significant results!

Unfortunately, negative self-talk is designed to make us feel bad that we're moving too slow or are not good enough. Now, imagine what would happen if we did it all the other way round? We would be unstoppable and so much kinder towards one another.

Extra exercises:

If you have more time to dive in, I highly recommend you start reflecting on how you talked to other people on the topic of their goals and ambitions.

Were you supportive? Negative? Cynical? Overprotective?

If you catch any negative patterns, ask yourself if you ever caught yourself using them while talking to yourself.

If yes, begin re-writing them. Remember, it's not about being overly optimistic or practicing the so-called toxic positivity while hiding your head in the sand. As already stated in this book, we all make mistakes. Sometimes we feel negative simply because some levels of negativity are needed to push us towards positive change or to learn, grow and appreciate the positive.

It's like being on a healthy diet and eating a pizza occasionally, not a big deal.
The problem is when we eat pizza or fast food, and it begins to define us. Well, same with negative talk towards others and yourself.

My guess is that if you ever catch yourself thinking negatively or speaking negatively towards others, it indicates that you still hold it within yourself and use it against yourself. If so, don't beat yourself up over it. Instead, be grateful and use it as a catalyzer or something that gives you feedback and information about yourself to learn and grow from it.

Since you are reading books like this one, and I'm pretty sure you have read many other books from people who are way more successful than I am, I know you value your growth and are always looking for new information and technique to create a better version of yourself.

Well, how you treat others always goes back to how you treat yourself. And how you treat yourself adds to your vibration and the signals you send out to the Universe. How you treat yourself leads to a specific set of actions that can either get you closer to or far away from your goals. If you keep telling yourself you will never succeed, chances are you don't even make any attempts to increase any probability of success.

Now, whenever you remember any situation where you weren't kind towards someone or were not supportive, don't beat yourself up. Simply re-write it on a piece of paper and in your mind. If you can, you can even apologize to someone and ask for forgiveness. I am sure they will appreciate it.

Yes, I know this exercise is not easy, and not everyone may be ready. But trust me, it's very liberating.

- Finally, the last exercise for today is to think of all the negative things someone else said about you, for example, that you were not talented, didn't have what it took, etc., and re-write it positively. If needed, use neutrality. For example:

Someone said:
"You are lazy, and you will never make it."
You can re-write it and say to yourself:
"Even though sometimes I fall off track, I still think I can succeed because I'm very passionate about this, and the more I do it, the more disciplined I get."

You can go as far as remembering some past situations and experiences from your life where you demonstrated patience and discipline. Always use your brain to look for positive proof and back it up with positive self-talk.

- Forgive those who said terrible things about you. Yes, I know, it's easier said than done, so if you're not ready, treat it as an additional exercise and get back to it whenever needed. It may take some time. But everyone needs to get started somewhere. For some of my readers, this may be the first step – understanding the importance of forgiving yourself and others and building some levels of awareness around this concept.

The first step is to write it all down and keep asking yourself if you're truly ready to let go and how your life would change if you simply could let it go.

What helps is compassion. How many times have you found yourself saying something negative (intentionally or not) simply because you had a bad day? We are all humans, and we make mistakes.

While in the process of forgiving, you can imagine people who hurt you with words, now apologizing to you and saying nice and supportive things to you. Be sure to add them to your own personalized mirror work!

When doing mirror work, embrace mindful experimentation. The only thing to keep in mind is to use positive and empowering words. Speak to yourself in the second person singular, for example, "You are doing great," as well as the first person plural, for example: "We are doing great."

The second option helps you ingrain a new, positive belief that you and your beautiful subconscious mind are a team and that you are working together. That one technique alone is priceless if you remember to do it regularly (at least once a day). Personally, I do my own version of mirror work whenever I can, that is, whenever I find myself in front of a mirror. All I can tell you is this – I wish I'd known about this earlier. And from my experience, the inner peace and kindness I have achieved while doing this technique is the best gift I could offer myself. I just wish everyone on the planet could experience such bliss and inner peace!

Day 4

The Courage to Be With Yourself without Having to Change Yourself

Have you ever experienced the power of disconnecting from everything and everyone just to be with yourself? It's exciting and scary at the same time. It's like going on a vacation with yourself while having the intention to disconnect from society as well as social media.

Some may think: "Oh, it must be so boring, what's the point if I can go on a vacation with a loved one and it's more fun?"

Yes, going on vacations with loved ones is fun, and there is a time for everything, but being with yourself is also needed, especially when it comes to tuning into your inner dialogues. Also, when you are by yourself, you have the advantage of saving your precious energy to use to get answers to your questions. The answers are within you. It's just a question of tuning in.

Imagine you go somewhere far away from civilization, and the only thing you can do is meditate, read, journal, or walk in nature. This is precisely what I did for a few days, and it was one of the best decisions I have made in my life. During that time, I read doctor Joe Dispenza's books, and I remember coming across a piece of interesting information (which I'm paraphrasing here): As humans, we tend to get addicted to negative emotions.

That really got me thinking about my own harmful addictions; one of them used to be talking to myself negatively. Yes, I was addicted to such rituals, and my thoughts, behavior, and actions would align with my addiction.

I also realized that by being all by myself and allowing myself a few days of simplicity, I reached some pretty amazing, positive and creative energy levels. I also experienced excitement knowing that I found such incredible joy in being with myself without distractions.

Our negative chatter often comes from rejecting a simple life and always looking for that next thing instead of simplifying our lives. For example, I used to be in the rat race, always chasing the next level and the next thing. I got burned out, and I thought quitting my job and becoming an entrepreneur would help me leave the rat race for good. Unfortunately, I also repeated the same pattern in my life as an entrepreneur, and so did many others. I kept running away from something, but that something was still inside me, and so I kept manifesting the same pattern, no matter what I did for a living and no matter where I lived.

Why? There are so many temptations. So many things to do, so many books to read, so many things to learn. And yes, I am all for reading, investing in myself, and growing.

But the moment we do it from a place of chasing, we begin to lose inner peace. And then, that negative internal chatter kicks in: "OMG, I am such a failure. At this stage of my journey, I should know this and make this amount of money. Others can do it; others are more successful. Something must be wrong with me."

Negative self-talk gets us on a never-ending path of looking for what's not working and getting stuck in a never-ending negative loop. So, once again, we keep asking ourselves: what's the next thing to do, what's the next thing to do on our to-do lists?

There's no "best next thing." The best next thing is going within by allowing yourself some time. Instead of being distracted by more things to do but ending up anxious and not knowing what to do while beating yourself up, you can replace distraction with going within yourself.

The external world can add to wanting to desire more and more while chasing more and more and just getting stuck in this chasing energy. Then, our self-talk goes in a self-defeat direction: "Oh, I'm not good enough yet; why is it taking so long?" But tuning into yourself adds to creating strong intentions while creating inner peace backed by positive and empowering self-talk.

To accomplish your goals, you need the unity of heart and mind, and this is only possible when you are at peace with yourself and can experience inner harmony.

You have fantastic powers already. However, you must use them correctly. If you carry on living in distraction all the time, you deplete yourself of your abilities.

(I say all the time because, in this day and age, it's absolutely normal to get distracted, and we can't escape it 100% unless we decide to become monks living on a top of the mountain, which, I imagine, most people can't do).

Chasing, being stuck in wanting, and fighting means that you are too fixed on your goals while actually separating yourself from them. This is especially true when your negative self-talk teams up with Miss Impatience. Before you know it, they both kick in with: "Why is this taking so long? I should have it now!"

But by allowing yourself to be with yourself, you can experience inner peace and calm while genuinely letting go.

You can immerse yourself in gratitude and reflect on how far you have come on this journey and how much you have learned. When you do this, an amazing thing happens, you begin to let go. And when you let go, you no longer feel needy and stressed. You begin to feel good. And when you feel good, you attract more and more good things into your life.

So, this is your exercise for today. Of course, I understand that not everyone can just go on a solo vacation to a far-away place for a few days. And that's absolutely fine. You can consider it as something to do and experiment with whenever you can. For now, ask yourself if you could do a mini version of disconnecting from everything?

Perhaps you can take a Sunday off? You can disconnect your phone and go hiking all by yourself or go to a local park. Or maybe you can wake up earlier and simply meditate in silence? Do whatever you choose to do. But trust me: the sooner you experience the power of disconnecting yourself from the world to connect with yourself, the more amazing shifts you will attract. The more you connect with your deep inner self, the more amazing answers you will discover.

Day 5

Making Friends with Your Subconscious Mind and Releasing Negative Patterns

This chapter will help you release negative patterns (such as overthinking, procrastinating, being negative towards yourself or others). By getting to the root of the problem, taking care of your self-talk will be so much easier. You will discover how to control your mind and unstick yourself from your old ways. You will finally create a powerful and peaceful space between you and your thoughts while letting go of negative patterns.

Before you learn how to control your mind, you need to understand how it works and what your problems may be.

You may have experienced the same negative patterns that keep coming up, so you feel like you are not making progress.

Old patterns are not just situations, but also compulsive habits, negative emotions, procrastination, and you just don't know why they all happen. All you know is you start beating yourself up and speaking negatively. The next thing you know is that your inner negative chatter opens a bottle of champagne and can't stop partying at your cost. Then, peace of mind seems almost unattainable.

It's like falling asleep unconsciously and having the same dream all over again. Then, the same feelings arise, and you don't feel good about yourself.

It's similar to a negative compound effect: something starts on a micro level, and we unconsciously rehearse it repeatedly while allowing it to grow.

Some people feel stuck in their careers. Whether they dream of increasing their income or venturing out to a new job, they feel trapped in their old identity and negative patterns.

As a result, the "I can't do this because I'm this and that" pattern starts invading their self-talk.

"I can't get a promotion because I'm too young, too old, or I don't have enough experience."

These can all seem like valid excuses because we really think we just are a certain way. We believe it's a fixed way, and we can't change it, at least not now. So, we get stuck in the energy of waiting and "not being able to for now." Then, we keep separating ourselves from our actual goals and desires while experiencing negative emotions about not even trying to change our situation. Negativity creates even more negativity, and we get stuck in a loop.

I've spoken to so many competent people about changing their situation because they have exceptional skills, talents, and characters. But, it always seemed almost impossible to encourage them to do something about their personal reality creation. They have been on an unhealthy self-talk diet for so long that they pretty much convinced themselves why they just can't reach their goals.

The exciting part is that our minds work like search engines. So, if you start looking for proof of why something is not possible for you, you will find it. Then, you can keep talking about it to yourself and others and create your reality based on why you can't do something and why everything always turns out so horrible. But, the good thing is that the same process also works the other way around – you can start asking yourself super empowering and positive questions that will lead you to the next level of success. Even if the process of getting closer to your dreams is long and complicated, you are still moving forward while celebrating every step on your journey. There's always a way out of negativity.

It all comes down to understanding how we handle different emotions and why we can get stuck in a negative loop.

According to David R. Hawkins (M.D., Ph.D.), there are different stages of processing negative feelings: repression, suppression, expression, and letting go. To learn more about his system, I'd highly recommend his book: *Letting Go: The Pathway of Surrender*.

Inspired by Doctor Hawkins' work, the following is my interpretation of various stages of processing our emotions in the context of learning how to power up our self-talk.

1. Repression – This one may seem to be the easiest at first, but unfortunately, it can negatively influence our lives. For example, something traumatic happens, and a person can't deal with it, so they repress such an event

unconsciously by burning it deep inside them and not even remembering it. This mechanism explains why we often unconsciously hold onto some old traumas that keep haunting us. Yet, we don't know why we keep attracting the same negative patterns because we can't even remember what started it in the first place. In this case, professional therapy can be really beneficial to dive deeper, face the past and heal.

2. Suppression is similar to repression, but it takes place on a more conscious level. Let's say something bad happens, and you don't want to deal with it. Maybe you are in a stressful situation or are very busy, so you get in a fighting mode while trying to save yourself.

You feel a painful feeling, but you choose distraction such as food, drinking, smoking, gambling, working, or whatever can help you not think and feel. The escape mode can also be scrolling on social media, watching TV, or playing games. Different people have different escape mechanisms. For me, it used to be drinking, partying, overworking, or scrolling. Sometimes, I still catch myself overworking, and I ask myself immediately: "Hold on, why do you think you should work more today? What are you escaping from?"

Overworking looks pretty innocent at first because we think we are productive. But, as with anything in life, balance is vital, and overworking as an escape mechanism can be very detrimental to our physical and mental health.

3. Expression is when we start complaining, gossiping, hating, or taking our anger or negative emotions out on someone else.

We may even think that letting it all out is good for us, but the tricky part is that it hasn't been let out entirely. It only managed to get expressed and probably amplified. It's like adding gas to fire!

So, expressed negativity always comes back to you anyway. Remember when we analyzed how talking negatively to others always gets reflected in our own inner dialogues? Or how people who don't treat you kindly most likely don't have high levels of kindness or compassion towards themselves?

So, expressing your feelings in a way that can hurt others in the end always comes back to us. Call it karma, consequences, or unfavorable circumstances. However, the good thing about it is that knowing what you know

now, you can play your own detective and use those situations as data to learn from. You can observe your own negative talk and self-talk and see what triggers it and why. Sooner or later, you'll start noticing many exciting patterns to learn from and improve your life.

I'd also like to add that expression is not always bad or negative. For example, you may choose to express yourself by confiding in a good friend, healer, therapist, or coach: someone who can help you. In such a case, you have a positive intention. You let it all out because you seek guidance, and you wish to heal. You know it's too much for you to process, and you decide to confide in an expert who can help you by analyzing your negative inner and outer patterns.

4. Surrendering and letting go is when you accept and allow whatever is happening. It's like observing instead of participating.

Surrendering is much more potent than escaping by suppressing, expressing, and behaving negatively towards others or spreading bad energy (not judging, I have done it many times!). Surrendering is the most powerful because it's fueled by love, not fear-based intentions.

But easier said than done. So many people grasp this concept and begin to focus on their thoughts, and thoughts can trigger different triggers in different people.

For example, the thought "I'm going to lose my job" may create stress and anxiety in some. But, some people may choose to think: "Well, even if I lose my job, I'll find a better one! I know that everything is unfolding just the way it should, to serve me and my bigger purpose."

It's essential to start practicing being honest with yourself by analyzing your thoughts and focusing on your feelings attached to them, not the thoughts themselves. A thought is just a thought, and it doesn't really mean anything on its own.

Simply unleash the feeling underneath your thought and approach it from a place of curious neutrality, as already discussed in the previous chapters.
Observation and acceptance are the best way to resolve old, negative patterns.

Let's say something happens in your work or business, and you experience feelings of fear, anxiety, failure, and guilt.

You have a choice now. How you respond or react to it.

Are you going to respond to it negatively? Or positively while truly believing everything will unfold for your highest good?

We often tend to get stuck in a duality of "this is good or bad," and we keep adding labels to everything while reacting with negative self-talk. Sometimes, we become way too attached to results. We literally fight for them or "trying to act positively" because we fear that something terrible will happen (so in the end, we are still negative inside as this is a fear-based emotion that makes us "try to be positive").

See everything as neutral and as yet another experience of life. Everything is a part of life, and we are here to experience contrast. This is probably one of the highest levels of inner peace you can achieve.

Getting too attached to what we (often with our limited awareness) label as good things can make us lose our inner peace or miss other opportunities that can work even better for us long-term. We love getting attached to things. We love to assume it will always be that way. Yet, we are not often willing to recognize that very often, life likes to test us or balance out our successes by other events that, even though at first may seem to be "failures," are needed for our ultimate growth and practice for the bigger show.

For me, personally, my most significant growth in life and business was through adversity. Although now, looking back at what seemed like "adversity" to me back then, I would actually call it a blessing because it helped me shape my character and skills.

What really matters is the journey. I recently talked to someone who became very successful. He confided in me that he actually started to experience more fear and insecurity after his first big success in business than when first starting out.

You see, when he was starting out, he didn't have that much to lose. But, after reaching massive success, he started to experience lots of fear of: "What if I lose it all and have to start from scratch?" So, he kept working more and more and more, which reverberated on his health and relationships.

It was only after realizing that he had to let go of his attachment to all his accomplishments and material possessions that he could finally experience inner peace, followed by more amazing achievements.

So now, his new mantra is: "Nobody can ever take away what's inside me and what I learned in the process of achieving success."

In other words, he knows that even if he lost it all, he could re-build himself fairly quickly, based on the practical and mindset skills he acquired on his journey. That simple shift in the way he talked to himself while letting go of old, negative, repressed, and suppressed emotions of "trying to prove something to others" gave him the peace of mind he was seeking. Now, he grows his projects because it gives him joy. He no longer acts from the fear of "losing it all" or "still feeling like a nobody."

Personally, I think that success without inner peace is not success but the rat race. And yes, I have been there too.

Accepting what could happen while cultivating inner peace is the best thing you can do to manifest your dream reality while remaining virtually unshakeable.

Exercise 1

Start practicing the art of acceptance and letting go by creating empowering affirmations using the following structure:

"Even though (add the situation or circumstance that may seem to be a bit negative), I choose to love and accept myself."

For example:
"Even though I didn't get that promotion at work, I choose to love and accept myself deeply and unconditionally."

Or: "Even though my book is not a bestseller, I choose to love and accept myself deeply and unconditionally."

Exercise 2

Find as many positives and lessons you learned as possible.

For example:

"Even though I didn't get that promotion at work, I choose to love and accept myself deeply and unconditionally. And I'm still very grateful I dared to put myself out there and have a go. Now, I've learned a lot about the company I work for, and I know I'm still moving forward. Besides, maybe the Universe thinks it's not the best time for me to get promoted? All is good in my world, and everything is unfolding just like it should."

Or: "Even though my book is not a bestseller, I choose to love and accept myself deeply and unconditionally. And, it's OK not to be a bestseller. The most important thing is to keep learning, writing, and serving my readers the best I can. I trust myself, and I trust the Universe. All is good in my world, and everything is unfolding just like it should."

Remember, you're just practicing for the bigger show. And, eventually, you always manifest what you practice - both internally, through inner work, positive self-talk, or visualization, as well as externally through actions you take to get closer to your goals.

Remember that you have the power to respond to everything. This is amazing. Whatever happens, even if you have no control over the event, you can control your reactions. Yes, I know it may be hard at first. It takes practice and perseverance. But it's possible. If you want to change the reflection in the mirror, you need to change the image first. The best way to change the image is to stop the race of desperately trying to change it but treat it kindly and with respect.

3. Write down whatever bothers you at the moment and mindfully choose and write down a positive response.

Your micro-actions, thoughts, and what you see through your own inner lenses create a compound effect that adds to your personal reality creation.

Day 6

Affirmation Mistakes to Avoid and the Secrets to Manifest Your Dream Reality with Personalized Affirmations

This chapter is all about creating your personalized affirmations that work while avoiding the most common affirmation mistakes to help you save time and energy.

Generally speaking, affirmations are positive statements that can be used to help you focus on what you desire and unleash positive possibilities and outcomes in your life.

But, following this simple definition without diving any more profoundly can make you stuck. For example, you may be tempted to pick some random affirmations simply based on the fact that they're created as positive statements thinking that now you're done.

And yes, in some cases, it may work. For example, you may be researching positive affirmations via books, blogs, or videos, coming across something you like, and just sticking with it and creating success. However, as sad as it may seem, most people never really succeed using such a method. Of course, listening to anything positive is always better than listening to negative, fear-based content. So, it's always a significant step to move forward and help you feel better while entering a more positive vibration.

However, if your goal is to use affirmations to get closer to your goals and create your dream reality, I highly recommend you dive a bit deeper and today's challenge is great for that! The good news is that after all the inner work you have done with this book, even what seems like a challenging task for most people will feel like a breeze to you!

My personal definition of affirmations is that they are very effective tools to help us align and be more resilient by unleashing positive focus. But, like anything else in life, they must be used correctly. In this case, when I say "correctly," I mean, "depending on your specific desires and circumstances." For example, what may seem to be the correct affirmation for me, may not be right for someone else.

So, if you ever felt frustrated thinking: "Oh, it doesn't work for me, or something must be wrong with me, maybe I'm full of bad energy and who knows what," don't worry, there's nothing wrong with you. Like many others, you may have been tempted to pick some random affirmations that perhaps worked for other people but not for you. The main reason being, they were not aligned for you and your specific energy.

You already know you need to choose your words very carefully. I write about affirmations in the final chapter of this book because I know that mastering the first steps outlined in this book is crucial if you are to succeed with your personal affirmations.

For example, when creating your affirmations, you need to use words that resonate with you, your desires, and your energy. Words have energy just like you do. And different words match different energies of other people.

For example, let's talk about affirmations to attract financial success. Some people really resonate with the energy of the word "abundance."

For example, I love the affirmation: "I attract unlimited and peaceful abundance in all areas of my life." When I say this affirmation, I immediately visualize unique and exciting images of feeling happy, healthy, surrounded by people I love, feeling fulfilled, and feeling financially free and stable, while enjoying everything life has to offer.

When I say "abundance," it also means balance in all areas of my life. Before I discovered inner work and the LOA, I was in situations where I could manifest financial success. Still, it being at the cost of other areas of life, my health, happiness, and fulfillment made me realize the importance of balance.

So, the word: "abundance" does it for me. Personally, it's not about multiple millions of dollars or expensive cars because those things don't resonate with me and my energy. When I say abundance, I can see myself at the beach with my loved ones, eating nice and healthy food, and celebrating success. I feel well taken care of by the Universe.

Some people, however, say "abundance" and don't really feel anything. Some people may prefer other words such as "money," or "cash," or "dollars." As for the last one, again, if your local currency is euro or UK pound, or something else, you may not resonate with the word "dollar". It may seem like something far away that people use on the other side of the world. But, if the dollar is your currency or you do business in dollars, it may make sense.

At the same time, some people I know, especially people who work in coaching, resonate with the word "impact."

A friend of mine uses affirmations such as: "Every day, I impact millions and millions of lives while reaching incredible success." It inspires her to create more content for her blog and social media, connect with her followers, coach people and grow as a leader. When she says "impact" deep inside, she knows that the more significant her impact, the more money, abundance, or dollars she can attract. So, it makes sense for her!

The same concept applies to manifesting pretty much everything in life. If you want to manifest love, ask yourself what you mean by "manifesting love." For some people, it may be getting married or finding their soul mate. For some, it may be attracting more exciting romance into their lives. For some, it may be a better connection with their family, spouse, or partner. Some people resonate with the word "love," some with "romance," "security," "feeling well taken care of."

As with everything related to inner work, the journey can be your destination, so give yourself some time to explore which words you feel really resonate with your energy.

When it comes to manifesting a healthy body, there are so many words you can use depending on what resonates with your soul.

Personally, I love: "I am full of unstoppable energy."

But, some people may prefer "I am healthy, slim, and fit," some may want to say: "I am toned," or "I am shredded." You need to dive deep and ask yourself what vibrant health really means to you and focus on words that reflect your energy.

It's also essential to make sure you believe in what you say. You want to create a connection with your affirmation. For example, if you keep saying, "I am a millionaire," but in your mind, even a 6-figure a year income seems like a far-away goal, you do not believe in what you say, and so you're losing trust in yourself and separating yourself from your destination. I'm not saying you should give up on your ambitions of becoming a millionaire or a 7-figure earner (see, just as another example, some people may prefer to say "a 7-figure earner" instead of a "millionaire").

So, back to manifesting massive financial goals such as becoming a millionaire or a 7-figure earner, whatever words may resonate with you more. You can still keep it as a goal. But, to believe in what you say, you may want to break your goal down and create an affirmation that you know you will believe in.

At the same time, you may want to immerse yourself in studying the minds of millionaires, how they think and how they perceive their reality. By taking such an action, your subconscious mind will slowly start to believe that becoming a millionaire is possible.

The only danger to avoid here is, when studying millionaires, you don't want to end up in a trap of comparing yourself to others while feeling negative and saying to yourself: "Oh, they could do it, but I can't because I'm this and that."

If this ever happens, make sure to go back to the previous chapters and re-do the exercises. Sometimes, it may be much more beneficial to say: "Even though I am not a millionaire yet in terms of dollars made, I am so happy and grateful I have the opportunity to study millionaires, how they think, and what they do because that alone makes my mind and soul so abundant!"

Let's take weight loss as another example. If a person is a couch potato for now, and on top of that, feels addicted to fast food, and just picks a random affirmation of: "Oh, I am so slim and fit, and I now reached my perfect weight," they may actually start feeling bad and not believe in what they say. I know because I've been there myself!

However, just like in our millionaire example above, they can also create an affirmation they believe in as their next goal. For example, if their current weight is 200 pounds, they may create an affirmation around something they believe in, such as weighing 180 pounds, and go from there. At the same time, they can also read about weight loss success stories to stay inspired and get in a mindset and energy of people who could lose weight and keep it off to stay close to the vibration of their next milestone.

Remember - always investigate your energy. How do you feel when saying your affirmation? Do you really believe it? While a little bit of stretch is fine as it can help you expand your comfort zone and focus on your new reality, be sure to avoid the trap of blindly reciting something that you don't honestly believe in.

The way I see affirmations - they can be a fantastic bridge to help us re-focus and take inspired action in alignment with what we want. They also help us program our minds for success and look for proof for achieving what we desire. You see, if we don't do anything and allow our minds to run on autopilot, most likely, we will start looking for proof as to why we can't have what we want.

Affirmations are a crucial piece of a puzzle. But, as already stated, there are also other pieces to take into consideration. It's about our mindset, energy, beliefs, how we treat ourselves from within ourselves, what kind of proof we look for, positive actions (for example, studying successful people), or negative (following gossip, negative press, or hateful media or speech).

I also believe that affirmations can really help you train your mind and discover what and how you feel when you do them. To me, affirmations are a bit like going shopping and trying out different outfits to see which one you like. As soon as you find the perfect one, you fall in love with it and feel like wearing it all the time. At the same time, at some point, you'll need a new outfit, and that's absolutely fine. We can always outgrow our affirmations or decide to change our style!

Below are more tips to help you create affirmations that work for you:

- Remember to use your affirmations in the present tense and avoid affirmations such as: "I want to lose weight," because, as already stated at the beginning of this book, "to want" means that you're in the energy of not having. To attract what you desire, you must be a vibrational match to it, so your thoughts, affirmations, and the way you speak to yourself and others must be of the person who already lives in your dream reality.

- Don't spread yourself too thin with your affirmations, as well as too many things to manifest. My personal recommendation is to focus on one or a maximum of two things at a time. It may also help if the two desires are interconnected. For example, having unstoppable energy and vibrant health can help you show up better in your job or business. So, in this case, it makes sense to focus on manifesting two things at once. At the same time, by manifesting more success in your job and business, you may raise your income which will allow you to buy quality foods or supplements to take care of your health.

However, super long lists of desires may produce scattered energy, and so there's no focus. Don't get me wrong; you can have a long list of long-term goals or things you desire to manifest. If you do, I'd recommend you create a vision board to remind yourself of how good your reality is yet to come. But when it comes to manifesting through affirmations, my personal recommendation is to focus on one or two things at a time. As they manifest, rinse and repeat. It's really lots of fun!

- Be aware of feelings of despair and losing patience; I know I know, easier said than done.

But here's the thing, sometimes, the Universe wants to test you, or occasionally, the timing is not right for you. By losing your patience, you also lose trust in yourself and your abilities. From time to time, it may be a good decision to change your path, and sometimes we don't manifest what we think we desired because there's something better waiting for us. The way the world goes, it's a perfect system. Do you get impatient waiting for the sun to come out? Of course not. You know that there are different cycles in life. Day and night. Summer and winter. For example, it takes nine months to give birth to a child. It's not that we can speed it up to one month with nine women instead of one. So, be patient, and enjoy the process. Ask yourself what you're learning and discovering. Every day, be grateful for the person you are becoming. Enjoy the view while mindfully climbing up your mountain of positivity.

- If needed, instead of "I," use "God," or "the Universe," or whatever power you believe in.

Some people will not believe in "I'm so powerful." instead, they prefer to say, "God is so powerful."

So, instead of saying: "I'm so powerful I always attract unlimited abundance," they may prefer to say, "God is so powerful he always helps me manifest unlimited abundance."

Choose whatever works for you.

Personally, I use both options. For example, when writing and creating, I love using the affirmation: "I feel the creative power of God and the Universe flowing through me." This affirmation makes perfect sense because when I write or create, I feel like I'm connected to something bigger than myself, and I feel like a co-creator. In other words, I give credit to the Universe and God because this is what I believe in, and this is what fuels my work.

Once again, it's totally up to you. But for many people, adding the higher power to their affirmations gives them more security and peace of mind, making them fully believe in what they desire to manifest.

- Get in a good vibe with music and exercise. Create a playlist with your favorite music, preferably the music and lyrics that make you feel good, so that you can get in a good and joyful mood before doing your affirmations. You may also want to move your body and exercise while doing your affirmations. In this case, I'd choose music and songs with no vocals so that you can entirely focus on your affirmations and use the power of music to uplift and energize you.

- Always write your affirmations down in different ways to check which one resonates with you. When you write your affirmations down, you are already manifesting them into physical reality, and isn't that alone super empowering?

- Keep your affirmations short and precise unless you feel good having long-winded affirmations that feel like reciting a poem.

Most people really benefit from shorter and more concise affirmations that are full of powerful and emotional words. But, as always, to each their own!

- Never use the negatives, for example: "I don't want to lose my job" because your subconscious mind can't understand "the don't," so all it hears is "I want to lose my job."

Unless, of course, for whatever reason, you want to manifest losing your current job, be sure to create your affirmations positively.

And, as you already know, don't use "want."

A much better affirmation would be:

"I have an amazing, stable, and well-paying job, and I love what I do."

Or: "I get paid well (or add how much money exactly you desire to manifest) while doing what I love and working with amazing and kind people."

There's always good in bad, though. If you ever find yourself in negative chatter such as "I don't want to manifest this and that," that it almost becomes your internal story or a negative affirmation, use it as data and turn it into a positive statement or affirmation.

For example, many readers tell me: "Oh Elena, but I don't know what I really want."

Then, I say to them: "I'm sure you know what you don't want, so use it as a starting point and flip it!"

At least, we can make some use of the negative if we act on time!

- Spice it up with emotion. For example, add: "I'm so grateful that," or "I'm so happy and grateful that," or "I love it."

For example: "I'm now making 10k a month working in my dream job with awesome people, and I love it!"

- Don't use other people's goals or success stories as your affirmations. Always double-check and screen your energy when thinking about your affirmation and a goal behind it. Do you want a bigger house just to impress others or because you think it is expected of you? Well, then maybe it's not really your goal? Perhaps you're happy living in a small apartment and manifesting something else?

At the same time, if thinking about living in a bigger house really sets your soul on fire, go for it!

- Put your affirmations all around you: your office, car, mirror, wardrobe, fridge, etc.

Don't hide them! Make sure you see them often and that they see you as well. They will help you stay resilient while taking care of your good mood and vibration.

Also, repeat them in from of the mirror, at least 3-4 times a day. By now, it shouldn't seem difficult or weird because you've already done your version of mirror work in the previous chapters (unless you didn't do your homework correctly, lol).

- If negative chatter kicks in while you're doing your affirmations, don't panic. Simply say "cancel, cancel" and carry on.

If negative chatter or images continue, I'd highly recommend you tap on yourself using EFT (Emotional Freedom Technique) to start eliminating blocked energy.

There are many excellent videos on YouTube that you can use to tap to start releasing old negative emotions and energies so that your affirmations and manifestation journey is more effective and fun. Personally, I am a big fan of tapping, and I tap on myself daily. I wish I'd discovered it earlier! But, hey, at least I can really appreciate the value of it now.

- Feel emotions around your affirmations and visualize them as you repeat them. How does it feel to experience your dream reality? Who do you share it with? Who's the first person you share your manifestation success with?

Visualization is a manifestation skill that I dive deeper into in my book, *Visualization Demystified*.

However, if you're new to this, don't worry. Simply relax and allow yourself the luxury of entering your dream reality. If you can't visualize, for now, focus on other senses, for example, smelling or hearing. Let's say your affirmation is: "I now live in a lovely 4-bedroom beach house, and I just love the sound of the ocean."

To support your affirmation and your new vision, you can start listening to the sounds of the ocean on YouTube or get in an "act as if" state by talking to yourself. "How about we have a nice cup of coffee while looking at the ocean?"

Then, you proceed to make coffee (in your current world) while already feeling as if you were in your new kitchen, in your new home, feeling excited about indulging in a nice cup of coffee after work, while enjoying the sound and smell of the ocean.

Remember, it's all about becoming the vibrational match to whatever it is you desire while embracing the process of who you're becoming and being grateful for every step on your journey.

Keep climbing that mountain of positivity. Mind your language because your words matter, and you can use them to be the conscious creator of your dream reality!

And yes, your challenge for today is to create your personal affirmation and use it as a bridge to practice resilience and courage to keep manifesting the next level of your dream reality! Your dream reality is already within you. I'm confident that going through this challenge will help you focus on the positive while reaching complete alignment of your thoughts, feelings, vibration, and actions.

Conclusion – Trust Yourself

Keep expanding and keep moving forward!
Watch your energy transform. Embody your desires. Be your desires. Affirm your desires with what you do and how you think about yourself, not only with what you say.

Don't get discouraged or impatient if it takes longer to manifest your desires; the journey itself is your destination. As you are exploring yourself and your manifestation abilities, you are becoming a better person. You are kind to yourself and others while cultivating a positive mindset infused with endless gratitude. That alone is a gift to those around you!

Keep practicing what you have learned, and keep sharing these concepts with others. Together we can change the world by collectively enhancing the vibration of the planet.

I genuinely hope that this book inspired you and gave you new tools to expand your consciousness and raise awareness.

You are limitless, you are powerful, and you are amazing! I believe in you and wish you all the best on your journey! If you have a few minutes, I'd really appreciate it if you could leave me a short review on Amazon. Let other LOA readers in our community know who this book can help, how, and why.

Thank You, Thank You, Thank You,
I hope we "meet" again,
Much love,

Elena

For more information and resources about LOA and manifestation, visit my website:

www.LOAforSuccess.com

If you'd like to say hi, please email me at:
elena@LOAforSuccess.com

Join Our Manifestation Newsletter and Get a Free eBook

To help you AMPLIFY what you've learned in this book, I'd like to offer you a free copy of my LOA Workbook – a powerful, FREE 5-day program (eBook & audio) designed to help you raise your vibration while eliminating resistance and negativity.

To sign up for free, visit the link below now:
www.loaforsuccess.com/newsletter

You'll also get free access to my highly acclaimed, uplifting LOA Newsletter.

Through this email newsletter, I regularly share all you need to know about the manifestation mindset and energy.

My newsletter alone helped hundreds of my readers manifest their own desires.

Plus, whenever I release a new book, you can get it at a deeply discounted price or even for free.

You can also start receiving my new audiobooks published on Audible at no cost!
To sign up for free, visit the link below now:

www.loaforsuccess.com/newsletter

I'd love to connect with you and stay in touch with you while helping you on your LOA journey!

If you happen to have any technical issues with your sign up, please email me at:

support@LOAforSuccess.com

More Books by Elena G. Rivers

Law of Attraction Short Reads Series

Money Mindset: Stop Manifesting What You Don't Want and Shift Your Subconscious Mind into Money & Abundance

How Not to Manifest: Manifestation Mistakes to Avoid and How to Finally Make LOA Work for You

Visualization Demystified: The Untold Secrets to Re-Program Your Subconscious Mind and Manifest Your Dream Reality in 5 Simple Steps

Law of Attr-Action for Entrepreneurs: Advanced Identity Shifting Secrets to Manifest the Income & Impact You Deserve

The Love of Attraction: Tested Secrets to Let Go of Fear-Based Mindsets, Activate LOA Faster, and Start Manifesting Your Desires!

Manifestation Secrets Demystified: Advanced Law of Attraction Techniques to Manifest Your Dream Reality by Changing Your Self-Image Forever

Script to Manifest: It's Time to Design & Attract Your Dream Life (Even if You Think it's Impossible Now)

Self-Image Demystified: The Proven Art of Attracting What You Want by Becoming What You Want

Now available in your local Amazon store (kindle, paperback and audiobook editions are available for your convenience)

www.ingramcontent.com/pod-product-compliance
Lightning Source LLC
Chambersburg PA
CBHW071403080526
44587CB00017B/3168